Skateboarding Competitions

Justin Hocking

The Rosen Publishing Group's
PowerKids Press™
New York

For Matt and Sean

Published in 2006 by The Rosen Publishing Group, Inc.
29 East 21st Street, New York, NY 10010

First Edition

Editor: Melissa Acevedo
Book Design: Elana Davidian
Photo Researcher: Gabriel Caplan

Photo Credits: Cover, pp. 1, 19 courtesy Vans; p. 4 © Elsa/Getty Images; pp. 7 (left), 12 (left) © Stan Liu/Icon SMI; pp. 7 (right), 8, 11 (bottom), 12 (right) Idaho Amateur Skateboard League, Inc., Loren Williams, photographer; pp. 11 (top), 15 Rob Meronek courtesy of Skatepark of Tampa; p. 16 © Harry How/Getty Images; p. 20 THRASHER / LUKE OGDEN.

Library of Congress Cataloging-in-Publication Data

Hocking, Justin.
Skateboarding competitions / Justin Hocking.— 1st ed.
p. cm. — (Power skateboarding)
Includes bibliographical references and index. ISBN 1-4042-3052-1 (library binding)
1. Skateboarding. I. Title.

GV859.8.H626 2006
796.22—dc22
2005000068

Manufactured in the United States of America

Contents

4 The 2002 X Games took place in Philadelphia, Pennsylvania. At the X Games, professional skater Eric Koston did a trick called a heel flip. During a heel flip, as shown above, a skater flips the board with his or her heel. Koston won third place in the contest.

The Importance of Skateboarding Competitions

Every year millions of people watch **professional**, or pro, skaters like Eric Koston take part in well-known skateboarding **competitions** like the X Games or the Vans Triple Crown. Skateboarding competitions are different than the other sporting events on television because of the conduct of the skaters. They care more about having fun than about winning or proving themselves. For this reason some professional skaters never enter contests. Instead they gain **recognition** in other ways, like having their pictures in skateboarding magazines.

Most pro skateboarders do enter contests because competitions are important. They give the skaters a chance to be seen by the public and also to win prizes. **Amateur** competitions are needed because they help younger skaters get noticed. If an amateur skateboarder wins enough contests, he or she may be offered a **sponsorship** by a skateboard company.

Different Types of Competitions

There are two main types of competitions. Amateur competitions give skateboarders who are still learning a chance to compete. Most amateur competitions have different **divisions** for beginner, **intermediate**, and advanced amateurs. Many amateur contests take place at local skate parks. Skilled riders take part in professional competitions. These contests are bigger events than amateur competitions. They usually take place in large open fields called arenas or skate parks that can hold many people.

Skateboarding competitions, whether professional or amateur, are broken up into two or three separate events. **Street-skating** events take place on courses with **obstacles** like **ledges** and **handrails**. **Half-pipe** events are held on large, U-shaped ramps. The most common type of half-pipe event takes place on a **vert ramp**. Some competitions also include a **bowl** event. Bowls have a round shape like that of swimming pools.

Professional skater Cara Beth Burnside does a trick during the women's bowl competition at the 2002 Vans Triple Crown. This competition was held in Oceanside, California. *Inset:* This picture of a skater sliding on a rail was taken at an amateur contest in Idaho.

Top left: In order to enter a skate contest, skaters have to sign up. *Top right:* They are then allowed to take a practice run. *Bottom:* After practicing, skaters take a 45-second run, which is timed by a timekeeper.

How Competitions Work

To enter a competition, the first thing you need to do is register, or sign up, for the event of your choice. Many skaters choose to enter more than one event. Most competitions charge between $10 and $200 for each event, depending on whether it is an amateur or professional contest. After signing up skaters are given a chance to practice. Practice is important because it helps skaters get used to the competition course or ramp.

The contest starts and skaters are given two 45-second runs, or chances, for each event. During a run the skater attempts several hard tricks in a row. If the skaters do poorly in the first run, they can make up for it in their second run. An announcer lets them know when it is their turn to skate and when their time is up. At the end the announcer names the winners and hands out prizes.

In a best trick event, skaters try one hard trick instead of a 45-second run. At the 1999 X Games, Tony Hawk won this event when he landed a 900 degree spin on a vert ramp.

Judging

Deciding who wins a skateboarding competition is an important job. It takes three or more judges, called a panel, to make these decisions. Judges are usually people with years of skating knowledge. The panel of judges for professional competitions is usually made up of **retired** professional skateboarders. For amateur contests judges are usually other amateurs who have been skating for several years.

During the competition judges pay close attention to each skater's run. They record the skater's score on a **judging sheet**. Scores are based on how hard the skater's tricks are, the skater's ability to stay on the board, and his or her overall riding style. Skaters are expected to do many different types of tricks in their run. They must also use the entire course or ramp. Judges choose the final winners based on the total score from the best of the skaters' two runs.

This panel of judges gets ready to judge a run during the Skatepark of Tampa's famous SPOT contest. *Inset:* This judging sheet is from an amateur skateboarding contest in Idaho.

After winning an event at an amateur contest in Idaho, this young skater receives his prize.
Inset: In the 2002 Vans Triple Crown Competition, Cara Beth Burnside won first place after her unbelievable moves in the women's bowl event. This picture shows her accepting the prize.

Prizes

Prizes are usually given to the top 10 or 20 skaters in each event. In amateur contests the winners sometimes receive **trophies**. Most amateur contests are also sponsored by several skateboard companies. These companies **donate** skateboards, wheels, hats, clothing, and stickers that are given to the top skaters as prizes.

In professional competitions skaters compete for large cash prizes. In 2003, the BOOST Mobile Pro Invitational Skateboard Contest gave more than $250,000 in prizes to winning competitors. The contest drew more than 40 professional skateboarders to compete in separate vert and street events. The first-place winner of each event walked away with $40,000. This was one of the highest-paying skateboard competitions in history.

Skatepark of Tampa Amateur Contest

Every January one of the most important amateur contests takes place at the Skatepark of Tampa in Tampa Bay, Florida. The SPOT Contest, as it is called, draws more than 200 amateur skaters from all over the country and the world. Some competitors come from as far away as France and Brazil to enter this contest. With so many skaters competing, the contest takes three days. Riders in each event must first compete in a **qualifying round**. The top 30 or so skaters then advance to the **semifinals**. Only about 12 of these semifinalists move on to the final round, where they battle it out for first place.

The SPOT Contest is important because the top riders often receive sponsorship from a major skateboard company. With the recognition they gain from the SPOT Contest, most first-place winners become pro skaters.

Many well-known professional skaters became pros after winning SPOT Contests. These skaters include Andrew Reynolds and Colt Cannon.

A skater grinds a handrail during the street-skating event in the SPOT Contest.
Inset: Companies sometimes donate enough to be given away to onlookers, not just the winners. This picture shows one such giveaway at a SPOT Contest.

The 2004 X Games was held in August at the Staples Center in Los Angeles, California. *Inset:* Winners of the 2004 X Games Skateboard Vert Best Trick event include, from left to right, Pierre-Luc Gagnon, Sandro Dias, and Danny Mayer.

The X Games

Every summer about 30 top professional skaters are invited to take part in a famous event known as the X Games. Millions of viewers watch the X Games on television. This includes people who would not normally attend a skateboarding contest. Television coverage makes the X Games the most well known of all the skateboarding contests. Along with featuring several skateboarding events, the X Games includes events for surfing and motocross. In addition to all the different sports, several rock-and-roll and punk rock bands play during the X Games to occupy viewers and contestants during breaks. As in the Olympics, the top three winners of each event are given medals. Medals are small, round pieces of metal that are given as prizes. Winners are also given cash prizes for as much as $50,000.

The 2004 X Games was held at the Staples Center in Los Angeles, California. Women's street and vert skateboarding competitions were held for the first time that year.

Vans Triple Crown Competition

Vans is the name of a company that has been making skateboarding shoes since the 1970s. Vans also holds the world-famous Triple Crown Competition for pros once a year. This competition consists of three separate events in three different cities. The first part is called the Slam City Jam. One of the biggest competitions in North America, the Slam City Jam takes place in the BC Place Stadium in Vancouver, Canada.

The next stop in the Triple Crown is Cleveland, Ohio, for the Built Ford Tough National Championships of Skateboarding event. The event is named after the sponsor, which is Ford. The top skaters then go on to the Vans World Championship of Skateboarding in Huntington Beach, California. The skater with the highest overall score from all three competitions wins.

Vans Triple Crown has 200 pro skaters competing for $100,000 in prizes. In 2004, Bucky Lasek won $18,000 and a brand-new Ford Ranger FX4 truck.

Bucky Lasek does a vert trick during the Triple Crown Competition. *Top inset:* Pro skater Tony Trujillo shows off his moves at the Triple Crown's Slam City Jam. *Bottom inset:* Bucky Lasek cheers after winning the Triple Crown Competition.

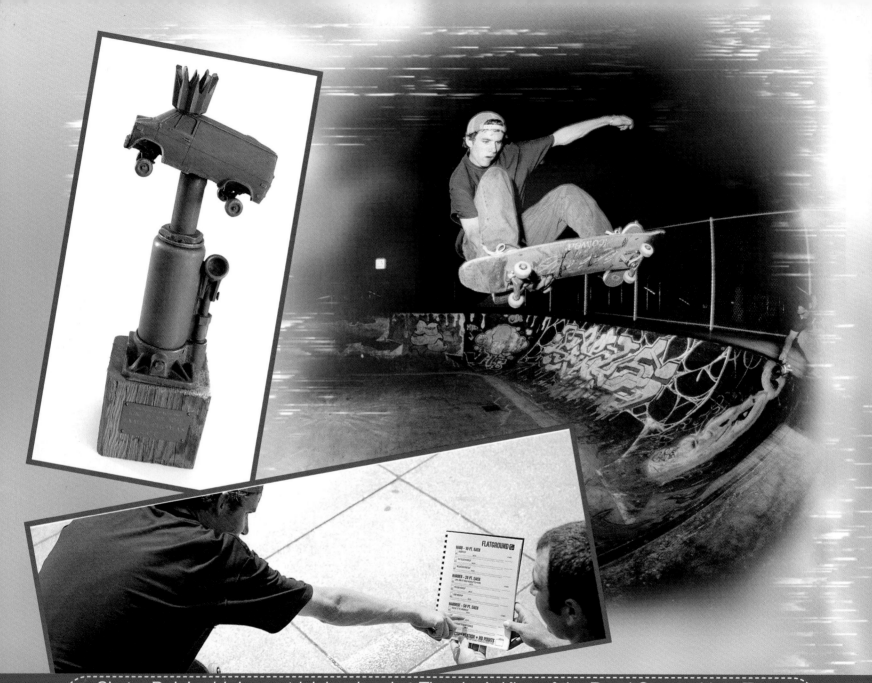

Skater P. J. Ladd does a trick in a bowl at *Thrasher*'s King of the Road Competition. *Top inset:* This is the trophy skaters get after they win *Thrasher*'s King of the Road Competition. *Bottom inset:* Skaters look at the judging sheet in order to plan out their next trick.

Thrasher's King of the Road Competition

Thrasher is one of the most well known skateboarding magazines. Once a year *Thrasher* holds a traveling competition called the King of the Road. The King of the Road is different from other skateboarding competitions. Instead of competing in one skate park, the competitors drive 4,000 miles (6,437 km) across America, skating in many skate parks along the way. This fun, weeklong journey begins in New York City and ends in California.

There are four King of the Road teams, which are made up of five pro skaters. At the beginning of the contest, each team is given a van and a list of tricks. Teams score points by visiting different cities and landing tricks at well-known skate parks. The tricks and traveling paths change each year. The team with the most overall points wins a King of the Road trophy and a cash prize.

No judges are on the road with skaters during the King of the Road, so all tricks must be filmed. Teams can win points doing fun things, such as landing tricks while blindfolded.

Tips for Entering Contests

Skateboarding competitions can be fun. They can also give you a chance to make friends with other skaters. Riding with skilled skaters can push you to do your best and to try new tricks. You also have the chance to win cool prizes.

If you like to skateboard, you might decide to enter an amateur competition. However, your first contest can be a little scary. If you are like most amateur skaters, you will probably get nervous skating in front of large groups of people. It helps to imagine the tricks you will try during your competition run. Pick moves that you feel comfortable with and know that you can land. Practice your tricks before the competition. Before your actual run, take some deep breaths and imagine landing every trick you practiced. Try to be calm and just have fun. Remember that you are not out to beat anyone or show off. Skateboarding competitions are about having a good time.

Glossary

amateur (A-muh-tur) Someone who does something as a hobby, for free.

bowl (BOHL) Like swimming pools, only deeper, bowls are used by skateboarders.

competitions (kom-pih-TIH-shunz) Games or tests.

divisions (dih-VIH-zhunz) Groups or departments.

donate (DOH-nayt) To give something away.

half-pipe (HAF-pyp) A ramp that is shaped like a big *U*.

handrails (HAND-raylz) Originally created to make walking upstairs and downstairs easier and safer, handrails are often used as an obstacle in skateboarding.

intermediate (in-ter-MEE-dee-et) A skill level that is between beginner and advanced.

judging sheet (JUJ-ing SHEET) A sheet that has the names of all the skateboarders in a competition event. Judges write down each competitor's scores on this sheet.

ledges (LEJ-ez) Small, square obstacles used for doing tricks.

obstacles (OB-stih-kulz) Objects that can be used in a skateboarding trick.

professional (pruh-FEH-shuh-nul) Someone who is paid for what he or she does.

qualifying round (KWAH-lih-fy-ing ROWND) An event held in a contest to see if a person is able to go on to the next event.

recognition (reh-kig-NIH-shun) Favorable notice and attention.

retired (ree-TYRD) Decided not to work or play a sport professionally anymore.

semifinals (SEH-mee-fy-nulz) Events held in a contest to see if a person can go on to the final event.

sponsorship (SPON-ser-ship) A person's or company's paying for and planning out an activity.

street-skating (STREET-skayt-ing) Having to do with skating in the street using obstacles like benches, stairs, handrails, and ledges.

trophies (TROH-feez) Prizes that are often made of metal and shaped like a cup.

vert ramp (VERT RAMP) The largest type of half-pipe, with walls that are completely vertical at the top. Most vert ramps are between 10 feet (3 m) and 13 feet (4 m) high.

Index

Web Sites

Due to the changing nature of Internet links, PowerKids Press has developed an online list of Web sites related to the subject of this book. This site is updated regularly. Please use this link to access the list:
www.powerkidslinks.com/skate/compet/

Mh.   10/06